MW01045311

O*pium_37*

O_{pium_37}

by Catherine Léger
with the collaboration of Éric Jean
translated by Leanna Brodie

Playwrights Canada Press
Toronto

Opium_37 © Copyright 2013 by Leanna Brodie
First published in French as *Opium_37*
French text copyright © 2010, Leméac Éditeur (Montréal, Canada)
All rights reserved

PLAYWRIGHTS CANADA PRESS
202-269 Richmond St. W., Toronto, ON M5V 1X1
416.703.0013 • info@playwrightscanada.com • www.playwrightscanada.com

For professional or amateur production rights, please contact:
Michael Petrasek, The Talent House
204A St. George Street, Toronto, ON M5R 2N6
416.960.9686, michael@talenthouse.ca

We acknowledge the financial support of the National Translation Program for Book Publishing for our translation activities, the Canada Council for the Arts, the Ontario Arts Council (OAC)—an agency of the Government of Ontario, which last year funded 1,681 individual artists and 1,125 organizations in 216 communities across Ontario for a total of $52.8 million—the Ontario Media Development Corporation, and the Government of Canada through the Canada Book Fund for our publishing activities.

 Canada Council
for the Arts
Conseil des arts
du Canada

 ONTARIO ARTS COUNCIL
CONSEIL DES ARTS DE L'ONTARIO

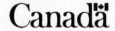 Canadä

 Ontario
Ontario Media Development Corporation

Cover photo © Laurence Mouton/ès/Corbis
Cover and book design by Blake Sproule

Library and Archives Canada Cataloguing in Publication
Léger, Catherine, 1980-
[Opium_37. English]
        Opium_37 / by Catherine Léger ; translated by
Leanna Brodie.

Translation of French play with same title.
ISBN 978-1-77091-177-2 (pbk.)

        I. Brodie, Leanna, 1966-, translator II. Title.
III. Title: Opium_thirty-seven. IV. Opium_37. English

PS8623.E46646O6513 2013   C842'.6   C2013-904406-X

First edition: September 2013
Printed and bound in Canada by Imprimerie Gauvin, Gatineau

Huge thanks
to Ian Lauzon
and to Diane Pavlovic.

Author's Note

This text began its life as part of a project initiated by Éric Jean in 2003 at the National Theatre School of Canada, a presentation by the students of the acting program that he directed called *Paris, 6 avril 1933*. I worked on the script with my colleague Alexandre Lefebvre, drawing on the writings of Anaïs Nin, Henry Miller, and Antonin Artaud.

In 2007 Éric expressed a desire to create another show, this time for Théâtre de Quat'Sous, centred around some of the characters from *Paris, 6 avril 1933*. He and I worked on the concept of an original piece that would distance itself from the texts of Nin, Miller, and Artaud while keeping Anaïs, Artaud, and June Miller as major characters. In 2008, working from this shared concept, I wrote the play you see before you.

Opium_37 is a work of fiction. Its inspiration is rooted in Nin's journals and in Artaud's body of work, but the script is neither historical nor biographical. It is, of course, a very humble attempt to pay homage to these two artists, but above all it's an endeavour to create something new, in the present tense, while reflecting on the aspects of their writing that remain fascinating to this day: the vast freedom, the sense of questioning everything, the boundless dissatisfaction.

*Opium_*37 was first produced in Montreal by Théâtre de Quat'Sous at Espace Go on November 25, 2008. It featured the following cast and creative team:

Paz: Kathleen Fortin
Anaïs: Évelyne Rompré
June: Eve Gadouas
Artaud: Daniel Thomas
René: Éric Paulhus
Fred: Stéphan Allard
Richard: Normand Daneau
Latimbrée: Martine-Marie Lalande
Germain: Yann Perreau
Zoe: Muriel Dutil

Director: Éric Jean
Set: Pierre-Étienne Locas
Costumes: Cynthia St-Gelais
Lighting: Martin Sirois
Music: Michel F. Côté
Hair and makeup: Angelo Barsetti
Stage manager: Nicolas Jobin
Assistant director: Annie Beaudoin
Apprentice director: Nathalie Piette

Characters

Paz: manager of the café
Anaïs: a character inspired by Anaïs Nin
June: a character inspired by June Miller
Artaud: a character inspired by Antonin Artaud
René: psychoanalyst
Fred: brother of Paz; coarse
Richard: paranoid artist
Latimbrée: mad poet
Germain: melancholy androgyne
Zoe: Dame Pipi*; prophet

---

* A Dame Pipi, once a fixture of Parisian life but now a rarity, is a professional toilet attendant. She cleans public restrooms and lives mostly off tips.

Prologue

ARTAUD sits in the shadows, a troubling glint in his eyes. Lights up on JUNE, who is magnificent. She has an American accent.

JUNE   Dear Anaïs.

ARTAUD   Dear Anaïs.

JUNE   I'm coming to Paris and I'm weary as hell.

She smokes.

ARTAUD   Perhaps writing to you now is a mistake.

JUNE   New York's killing me.

ARTAUD   I just got out of a cruel place where they wanted to detoxicate me.

JUNE   You won't believe what I've been through over there. I'm dog tired, Anaïs.

ARTAUD   I see so clearly. So... so horizontally straight that my comprehension of the world suffers for it. And I think about you.

JUNE   Kept thinking about you. Been three years, now.

ARTAUD   Your frail deceiving face keeps coming back to me. And I want to find you again, after months, after years.

JUNE   I think of those perfect moments we made together, you and me. The euphoria, the madness...

ARTAUD   I need the fog that floats around you. I want to be dulled, blunted. Sedate me with lies and carnal obsessions.

JUNE   I want to be with you again, Anaïs, you and the lace around your neck, the jewels on your fingers, the flowers on your dress.

ARTAUD   I want your criminal green eyes.

JUNE   I'll be at the Café de la Gare, tomorrow.

ARTAUD   Tomorrow, I'll be at the Quai d'Orléans.

JUNE &
ARTAUD   I'm waiting for you, Anaïs.

1.

A Paris café in the 1930s. PAZ *is washing glasses.* ZOE, *seated at a table, checks the time.* FRED *arrives from the back room, a pistol in his hand.*

FRED   Guess what I just found, again?

PAZ   Give it!

PAZ tries to get the pistol, but FRED holds it out of reach.

FRED   A pistol! And where did I find this pistol?

PAZ   Fred!

FRED   In the kitchen!

PAZ   It's mine!

FRED   I told you to stop hiding pistols all over the place.

PAZ   Give it!

FRED   But no. You never listen.

PAZ   It's my café. I'll do as I please.

FRED   It's *our* café.

PAZ   I'm the one who takes care of everything.

FRED   What do you want? You want ME to start washing
           dishes? I am the head of the family!

PAZ   Head of the family?

           She laughs.

           There is no family anymore. There is no head.

FRED   Big brother plus bastard little sister equals family,
           whether you like it or not. I'm the oldest. I am the
           head and you will stop hiding pistols all over the
           place!

PAZ   I'm sick to death of you. To death.

           FRED *searches the café and finds pistols.*

FRED   Another one. Another one... Absolutely crazy. You
           get that from your father.

PAZ   Don't talk about my father.

FRED   He was a real shit, your father. A fraud. Wasn't even a real Spaniard. They called you Paz to make you believe you were Spanish. So you'd be a fraud too, just like him. That's why you're crazy. Because of your father.

> *He throws the pistols on the ground.* PAZ *watches him, powerless.*

He was a real pig. I know. I was there the night they had you.

PAZ   You were two years old!

FRED   Mama was in pain. She screamed and screamed. And now, here you are, and you love pistols. Because you want to scream, too. Make a big *pow*. But you're too little a girl to make a big *pow*.

PAZ   I'm not a little girl.

FRED   A frustrated little girl... And it's up to me to protect you from yourself. From your own dreams of violence.

PAZ   It's nothing to do with dreams. It's the opposite. I'm a realist. I see what's happening, I feel it. And when I need a pistol—because even though you don't realise it, things are changing, everywhere, something is coming—

FRED   —That's the old lady putting ideas in your head. You're not a realist. You're just alienated.

PAZ   You can't understand. You're too soft. You don't even like pistols.

> FRED *stops hunting for pistols and looks at* PAZ, *insulted, a pistol in his hand.*

FRED   Me? Me? I don't like pistols?

PAZ   Yes. You.

> *He fires a shot in the direction of* PAZ *and deliberately misses.*

FRED   Wrong: I love pistols!

> *Second shot.*

I'm crazy about pistols!

> *Third shot.*

It's your craziness I don't like.

> FRED *gathers up the pistols and leaves.*

PAZ   Leave me one, at least.

               PAZ, *furious, punches the bar. Then she disappears into the back room.*

2.

At the café, a little later. PAZ returns from the back room with a leather bag from which she takes more pistols. She washes the pistols just as she washed the glasses. ZOE, still seated in the same spot, checks the time patiently. ANAÏS and RENÉ enter the café.

RENÉ   You disappoint me, Anaïs. You disappoint me greatly.

ANAÏS   *(sighing)* That's exactly the tone I was talking about. That ever-so-slightly paternalistic tone… it's unbearable.

RENÉ   *(paternalistically)* You are rebelling against me, it's only to be expected… during the psychoanalysis, a patient transfers a great deal of power to the therapist and this can have the effect of creating a sentiment of having been… alienated… diminished… It creates anger.

        Then, more softly for propriety's sake, incapable of concealing his pride:

        Passion, too… Look how crazy we are about each other.

ANAÏS   All those sessions in your office when you didn't say a word... It was so...

RENÉ   Erotic?

ANAÏS   Restful... Admit it, things were much better when I was doing the talking.

RENÉ   Obviously—you can't stand being contradicted.

ANAÏS   You mean to say "controlled."

RENÉ   You are incapable of sacrifice, incapable of repressing a desire, however slight.

ANAÏS   To see June again is not a "slight desire." It's not even a desire. It's a necessity.

RENÉ   You cannot refuse to meet with Artaud.

ANAÏS   I don't see how this concerns you.

RENÉ   When Antonin Artaud asks you to go and meet with him, you go.

ANAÏS   I admire Artaud greatly... but from a distance. Our little affair was so complicated, sad and complicated...

RENÉ   But things have changed... That was years ago.

ANAÏS	Exactly. I don't understand what he wants from me now.
RENÉ	Do it out of friendship for me. For us.
ANAÏS	If I go to see Artaud, it will be for Artaud. I do things for their own sake, not to please…

RICHARD comes into the café, a manuscript in his hands. He sees RENÉ and points at him.

RICHARD	You…
RENÉ	*(surprised)* Me?
RICHARD	Plagiarist. Rotten plagiarist.
RENÉ	Richard, calm down.
RICHARD	One week ago, the good doctor here tells me, "Richard, I'm writing a novel, just for a lark, in my spare time; I don't know if anything will come of it—"
ANAÏS	—You? You write?
RENÉ	Oh! Writing: it's one thing to talk about it… It's only a first attempt.
RICHARD	Out of the goodness of my heart, I tell him, "René! My friend, you've written a novel. How wonderful."

I offer to help him, without hesitation. Everyone knows I am well acquainted with several publishers... I tell him, "If you like, my dear René, I could read your book and, when the time is right, pass it on to the right publisher." Imagine my surprise on discovering that this novel isn't even yours!

RENÉ   What?

ANAÏS   *(enjoying herself)* You're so clinical. So devoid of imagination. It's a little surprising that you would write, don't you think?

RENÉ   Anaïs, please...

ANAÏS   Is it inspired by your patients?

RICHARD   This novel is mine.

RENÉ   *(to RICHARD)* Nonsense!

RICHARD   Page after page, after page, after page. Mine!

RENÉ   That's ridiculous: you haven't written anything for months.

RICHARD   I was about to write! I was just going to start. I'd thought it all through. You stole my novel from me before I'd even written it. Psychoanalyst? Bollocks! You are a voyeur and a thief.

RENÉ   Preposterous… How can I steal something that does not yet exist!

ANAÏS discreetly leaves the café, attempting to escape from RENÉ.

RICHARD   That's what I thought, too, but this…

He holds up the manuscript.

This proves otherwise.

RENÉ   Anaïs! Anaïs! Where are you going!

To RICHARD, his heart no longer in it.

That's nonsense, you know. It really is.

RENÉ goes off in pursuit of ANAÏS.

RICHARD   Thief! Dirty plagiarist!

He picks up a glass, making as if to throw it. PAZ loudly clears her throat. He sees her, stops dead, adjusts his hair, and immediately shifts moods.

Hello, Paz. How are you today?

PAZ smiles politely and continues to wash the glasses.

3.

In the street.

*FRED sets down the bag full of pistols and knocks
at a door.*

FRED   Anyone there? I have things to sell.

He knocks harder.

Come on! Open up!

*He picks up his bag and is about to leave when
LATIMBRÉE appears.*

LATIMBRÉE I have the loveliest ankles in Paris and I need two
hundred francs.

FRED   Too bad they're not worth it.

*FRED tries to go on his way but LATIMBRÉE
blocks him.*

LATIMBRÉE   I can sell you my hands, my mouth, my thighs—open them and close my eyes.

FRED   Well, me too: I can sell you my hands, my thighs—clench them and so on and so forth—

LATIMBRÉE   —My legs are doors that open and close. My lips are sluices that keep the water of my mouth from falling at your feet. No one sets foot on the water of my mouth. Not without paying. If you pay, I will give you all my liquids. I need two hundred francs.

FRED   Leave me alone.

LATIMBRÉE   I know men by heart. I know all the vices. I take care of a man as I clean a basin: while reciting poems and holding my breath. Once, a man paid a thousand francs to touch my ankles.

FRED   A thousand francs?

> FRED *looks at her ankles, perplexed. He circles her, intrigued.*

I don't understand.

LATIMBRÉE   I am an incredible woman. I recite poetry. Here, I'll do you one for free. On the spot. Just to give you an idea.

FRED   That won't be necessary.

LATIMBRÉE On a sunny afternoon one day
           I saw God on the Champs-Élysées
           With a frog leg where his heart should be
           He jumps 'twixt hell and heaven easily
           Not like poor old human us
           Condemned to carry our hearts full of pus
           God he gambols in the street
           With his odd-shaped sex and his horse's feet
           Humbling men who beg him Please
           We beseech you on our knees
           Mercy God give us a heart
           Give us an ungodly heart

FRED   Not bad.

LATIMBRÉE Two hundred francs and I'll do you a recital while
           you mount me: it's utterly delightful. You'll see.
           And I don't know if it's me or the poetry, but having
           once tasted me, men become dangerous. I have
           been told that men who have screwed me should
           be destroyed as you destroy a beast that has tasted
           human flesh.

           He thinks, then shows her what's in the bag.

FRED   I've got pistols. You can choose one, or even two. Go
           on, take two—

LATIMBRÉE —No, that's no good… Paying me with pistols? Are you morbid or something? Never mind. I'll go try somewhere else.

FRED No, wait. I'll find the money. Wait for me here. I'll be back.

FRED goes off with his pistols.

LATIMBRÉE That's right: that's right. Everyone comes back here sooner or later… It's just like the Eiffel Tower. Go on, goodbye!

She goes off immediately.

I have the loveliest ankles in Paris.

4.

On a quay.

ARTAUD *is standing hidden in the shadows.* ANAÏS
and RENÉ *enter but do not see him.*

ANAÏS   So now you're following me?

RENÉ   I'll keep you company, if you don't mind—

ANAÏS   —Honestly, I ask myself what you're playing at. Are
you using me to please Artaud? Or are you using
Artaud to control me?

RENÉ   I am simply trying to be a good friend to one and all.
A peacemaker.

ANAÏS   It doesn't suit you.

RENÉ   You are harsh with me, evasive. I know you, Anaïs.
Always in search of the next passion.

ANAÏS   You didn't mind that when the next passion was
         you... Artaud's not here, I'm going to meet June.

         ARTAUD comes out of the shadows.

ARTAUD   I was here well before you.

ANAÏS   Artaud...

         *ANAÏS stares at ARTAUD, visibly uneasy. ARTAUD cir-
         cles her, ensorcelling her.*

ARTAUD   I just got through a difficult hospital stay. My head is
         clear. Too clear. And I thought that in seeing you I
         would find myself again. Obviously I was mistaken.
         I wanted fog. But if you have somewhere else to be—

ANAÏS   *(sincere)* —I'm here now.

ARTAUD   No, you are not encompassing me. You are elsewhere.

ANAÏS   Not anymore.

ARTAUD   So you're here, are you? Really. And you, René?

RENÉ   I was just leaving.

ANAÏS   No, stay. We're among friends; isn't that right,
         Artaud?

ARTAUD   You are a chameleon, Anaïs. You always transform yourself exactly in relation to the surrounding spermatology. Let him stay then, if that's what you want. He will be a buffer for our clashing consciousnesses. A form of thrift.

ANAÏS   *(coming closer to* ARTAUD, *gently)* The hours we spent together. They were absolute, don't you think? Our proximity was mad and unbearable, sheer symbiosis…

ARTAUD   It was a few brief moments, some minutes.

ANAÏS   Marvellous minutes that you destroyed with your uncontrollable hatred. And those minutes are why you wanted to see me today: you felt a need for the absolute.

ARTAUD   Minutes, minutes, minutes, which, the moment they were consumed, were lost in the flow of your unstable hours. Either you are always in search of new prey, or, from one man to the next, you offer yourself with the sole aim of cramming yourself with yourself. For you nothing counts except pleasure and the telling of it.

ANAÏS   For you everything is a wound. There's nothing I can do. Nothing anyone can do. You love to double over with pain.

ARTAUD   You can't stand me because I'm the only one who's
          not ensorcelled by you. Your criminal green eyes. I
          read you, Anaïsssss.

ANAÏS   Well, stop it. It's exhausting.

ARTAUD   It's stronger than me. I must protect myself from you.
          Because you are an ingrate.

ANAÏS   Me? What about you? Excessive egocentric!

ARTAUD   Esoteric eroticist.

          ANAÏS *and* ARTAUD *hurl insults at each other,*
          childishly, while RENÉ, *caught between them, is*
          simultaneously fascinated and panicked.

ANAÏS   Loudmouth la-di-da piss artist!

ARTAUD   Vacillating lesbian.

ANAÏS   Yellow-bellied mystic.

ARTAUD   (*drawing out his esses*) Venomouss sserpent.

ANAÏS   (*imitating him*) Galactiiiiiiic ssousse.

ARTAUD   Unsssscrupuloussssssss ssssssssssssssluuuuuuuuuuuut.

ANAÏS   You're incredible, Artaud. Always suspicious. Always
                 threatened. And yet you're the strongest of us all.

ARTAUD   I see through people. The wickedness. The constant
                 betrayal. And the emptiness. People are empty so
                 they want to take everything. I don't know anymore
                 why I wanted to see you so badly. And yet, I really
                 did want to. But with you everything is always too
                 clear. And I need fog. *Adieu.*

RENÉ   No! Artaud!

                 (to ANAÏS*)* Now look what you've done!

                     ARTAUD *leaves.*

ANAÏS   I've done nothing. Nothing.

                     ANAÏS *leaves.* RENÉ, *confused, watches them go off*
                     in opposite directions.

RENÉ   Anaïs! Artaud!

                     He hesitates, then at last goes off in pursuit of
                     ARTAUD.

5.

At the café. PAZ *plays with her pistols.* ZOE *is seated at the same place as always, silent, patient.* RICHARD *is lolling over the bar.*

RICHARD   It's awful, Paz; they persecute me, they steal from me. I'm devastated, that's what I am. Completely devastated.

PAZ   *(mocking)* Yes, Richard. Like last time with that cabaret artiste—

RICHARD   —Exactly. You remember! All of his songs were mine.

PAZ   And that other one, you know, the painter—

RICHARD   —Who had the gall to try to sell me a painting he'd stolen from me, every inch.

PAZ   *(playing with him)* You know what I would do, if I were you. I would avenge myself on all these artists who are always stealing your work—

RICHARD   —Yes, good idea. But how?

PAZ   Stop creating. Stop thinking. And a few months from now, you'll see them, those thieves. They'll all be standing around… completely out of inspiration.

RICHARD   Yes, yes. I will deprive them of my genius till it kills them. All of them.

      He stops, thinks.

      No, wait. How am I supposed to stop thinking? How am I supposed to stop creating?

PAZ   I don't know… Do something else.

RICHARD   You think I'm not really a poet? That I'm not an artist? What you're asking me is not something you ask of a real artist. An artist can't stop creating. It's stronger than him: an artist creates without even realising it, all the time.

      He looks at PAZ, *outraged, crushed.*

      You don't believe in me.

PAZ   Sure I do—

RICHARD   —No—no—

PAZ   —Come on, Richard.

RICHARD   *(hurt, prideful)* I'll show you what I'm capable of.

              RICHARD *leaves.* PAZ *sighs, continues to wash the glasses.*

ZOE   Noon.

              PAZ *looks at the time, leaves off what she was doing, pours a glass of port, and serves it to* ZOE, *mechanically.* ZOE *drinks the port.*

Commentary for June 22, 1937. Yesterday, Léon Blum of the Popular Front resigned the presidency of the French government because he has been prevented from taking the necessary steps to counter the rise of the far right… The catastrophe is so close now it blinds your eyes and splits your heart. Oh well. Who's going to believe an old toilet attendant—a Dame Pipi? Even though thirty-five years as a Dame Pipi sure brings you close to the human race. I've learned everything I know cleaning other people's piss… I look at other people's piss and I can read the future! I see women, humiliated, their heads being shaven… I know the bombs will be here soon, and for a long time. I'm repeating myself. But you've got to repeat yourself, anyway, because either people aren't listening or they don't remember. It's not like I'm trying to upset you, no. If I wanted to upset you

I'd tell you: go open the cemeteries, go dig mass graves. No, I don't want to upset anybody. I'm going to die on April 20, 1941. I know the history of the world. But after death, I don't know. That's not my area. That's for the dreamers.

> ZOE *is silent.* PAZ *keeps on washing glasses and pistols.*

6.

In the street.

*GERMAIN, a very dandyish androgyne, is pulling
JUNE by the arm. They are drunk. GERMAIN is singing a love song. JUNE tries to join in but mostly
mumbles instead… Then she stops, shattered.*

JUNE   Time is it?

GERMAIN   Don't know anymore.

JUNE   Gotta get to the café, I'm meeting someone—

GERMAIN   —Stay with me.

JUNE   Another time, sweetheart.

GERMAIN   Kiss me. You promised me a kiss.

JUNE   I'm all woozy… Feels like I been kissing everyone
all night.

GERMAIN   You didn't kiss anyone.

JUNE   Really? But—

GERMAIN   —All night you kept promising kisses to everyone, especially me. But you didn't kiss anyone.

JUNE   To you?

     She laughs.

     You like kissing women, do ya?

GERMAIN   I like promises kept.

JUNE   *(circling him)* I thought you kept up this racket to trick men at night when they're drunk. You wanted us to pick up men, together, I thought.

GERMAIN   Picking them up is one thing. You enjoy driving them mad.

JUNE   I've driven men mad?

     She bursts out laughing, seductively.

     How many?

GERMAIN   I'd say... a dozen.

JUNE   You're making that up.

            She tries to go. GERMAIN *holds her back.*

GERMAIN   Let me kiss you.

            GERMAIN *tries to embrace* JUNE *but she slips away
            from him.*

JUNE   No.

GERMAIN   You're so beautiful.

JUNE   You like men and I'm a woman.

GERMAIN   You're different. Virile and fragile. Like me. I want
            to lose myself with you.

JUNE   You're drunk. People love me when they're drunk. I
            am intoxication. Where booze leaves off, June still
            burns bright. Hold on to that illusion. And I'll kiss
            ya later. Or not.

            LATIMBRÉE *enters, sees* JUNE *and* GERMAIN,
            *approaches. They're too absorbed to notice her
            coming.*

GERMAIN   Now. Kiss me right this second. Just a kiss. Just one.
            Give me breath, June.

> JUNE *lets herself be tempted, comes closer… But*
> *they are interrupted by* LATIMBRÉE.

LATIMBRÉE   I live in a closet. My legs are doors that open and close. My lips are sluices that keep the water of my mouth from falling at your feet. If you pay, I will give you all my liquids.

GERMAIN   We don't have any money. Let's go, we're late.

JUNE   *(to LATIMBRÉE)* You've got a swell voice.

LATIMBRÉE   That's nothing. For two hundred, I'll level all of Paris with poems, ass in the air—

GERMAIN   —You're going to be late for Anaïs.

JUNE   Wait.

LATIMBRÉE   Life is an equation that doesn't work. On one side of the equation: figures. On the other side: more figures. But they never add up.

GERMAIN   June—

JUNE   —I like to count in French. Figures are beautiful, in French.

LATIMBRÉE   For *deux cent*, I'll count up to *six cent vingt-huit*. I'll even give you *sept cent quarante-quatre* for free. *Trois.*

Soixante-douze. Cinq cent quatre-vingt-sept. I count and the sidewalks disintegrate. I bring you back to the street. And I say two hundred. *Deux cent.* No, wait: for you, *deux cent quatorze,* because it has a nice sound.

GERMAIN   We haven't got any money.

LATIMBRÉE   No one's ever got the money to pay me. That's my problem. It demands great strength of character not to lower my price. The worst of it is, there's never any clients around when you really want a screw. Oh, well. Got to look on the bright side: at least you stay clean while you're waiting.

JUNE   I like numbers. They glide. Don't say anything. Don't let themselves be hoarded. I don't like hoarding things. I like to have everything and lose everything.

LATIMBRÉE   *Deux cent quatorze.* And I'll recite poems.

> JUNE *takes off the necklace she is wearing and puts it around* LATIMBRÉE's *neck.*

JUNE   Don't like poems. I like numbers. They're more true.

LATIMBRÉE   *Huit. Trois cent vingt-huit. Huit et dix-sept.* I'd like to disappear. *Neuf et deux encore. Quatre deux. Trois sept.* Life counts itself inside our ears. *Vingt. Un.*

Trente. I'm up to my armpits in numbers. *Quatre.*
Six. Vingt-deux.

GERMAIN   Come on, June.

        GERMAIN *pulls* JUNE *away with her.*

JUNE   *(to* LATIMBRÉE*)* Thank you!

LATIMBRÉE   *(taking off the necklace, examining it)* All of them—mad.

7

At the café.

PAZ *takes a glass to* ANAÏS.

PAZ	Champagne for Madame. I'd love to know how anyone can feel like celebrating these days.
ANAÏS	I'm expecting someone, and that makes me happy.
PAZ	As you wish. If you want to be happy, be happy. Personally I find it a little undignified, but to each his own.

RICHARD *enters, hiding something behind his back.*

RICHARD	Here I am! It's me!
PAZ	*(unenthusiastically)* Oh, look: an artist.
RICHARD	Yes, Madame. Our Richard! I would go so far as to say, our amazing Richard! Has concocted us an

inspired work carried out in collaboration with God himself in person. Producing the most dazzling and stirring result—

PAZ   —Enough, Richard, we understand.

> RICHARD *takes a bouquet of flowers from behind his back.*

RICHARD   It's for you.

> RICHARD *is in love.* FRED *arrives, slamming the doors.* PAZ *grabs the bouquet from* RICHARD's *hands to hide her pistol.*

FRED   I need two hundred francs.

PAZ   Why?

> FRED *rummages through a small cupboard looking for money, finds nothing but a few coins.*

FRED   So I can have some fun, why do you think? I spend all my time putting up with your moods. I need to let off a little steam—

PAZ   —Two hundred francs? That's ridiculous.

FRED   Give it anyway!

PAZ   Don't have it.

FRED frisks PAZ, finding a fifty-franc note.

FRED   Fifty! It's a start... And our rich writer'll make a little donation... Right, Anaïs?

He presses himself on her, brazenly.

ANAÏS   Go to hell, Fred.

FRED   She's crazy about me...

Heads toward RICHARD.

Richard!

RICHARD *(intimidated by FRED)* Yes?

FRED   I need you.

He shows him the fifty-franc note.

Change this fifty for me.

He takes a bulging bill clip from his pockets, still intimidated.

RICHARD Certainly... You know me. Anything to be useful.

> FRED *takes the bill clip from* RICHARD'*s hands and very rapidly, in order to rattle him, counts while depositing the bills on the table.*

FRED   So… A ten note, plus a ten note, plus a ten note, plus a twenty note… That's fifty.

RICHARD   That's right.

> FRED *makes the exchange.* RICHARD *goes to take the pile of bills, but* FRED *stops him.*

FRED   Wait, no, that's not right… What do you say I take back my fifty note and instead you give me two twenty notes and two ten notes because otherwise that's a lot of bills. Besides, I'll probably lose them, you know me—

RICHARD   —Yes, yes, the fewer ten notes the better.

FRED   *(taking the bills)* So this time, instead, two twenty notes and two ten notes—

RICHARD   —Uh… Yes, yes, all right—

FRED   *(taking back the fifty-franc note)* —Unless I take back the fifty note and give you back the ten notes.

> FRED *speaks very quickly, handling the bills very quickly.* RICHARD *is hypnotised.* FRED *fills his pockets:* RICHARD'*s bill clip is emptied.*

And you know what? The thing is, you can never have too many ten notes, so I'll give you back a twenty note and take back my four ten notes… Unless I keep the twenty note, leave you two ten notes and you give me back instead another fifty note… or two… yes, two, plus your ten notes, gets us to fifty! That'll do it.

    RICHARD *is truly confused.*

And here's a little surprise for you… on the house.

    FRED *takes a bill, makes a paper bird with it, and gives it to* RICHARD.

RICHARD   Oo! A bird!

    FRED *goes off, his pockets full.*

FRED   Bye, all!

RICHARD   *(servile, content with his bird)* Bye, Fred!

ZOE   One o'clock.

    PAZ *serves a port to* ZOE. RICHARD *looks at* ZOE *in anguish.*

The great thing about port is it wakes up the palate. Léon Blum said, "Sometimes poisons are remedies: certain poisons however are only poisons."

Pause.

But why do they exist, then—these poisons that are only poisons? What good are they? Why should nature be wicked that way? What is it trying to prove? In Spain, at Guernica, they kill civilians by the ton. In Italy, you can't even talk to your neighbour anymore without getting yourself arrested. And in Germany… It's too ugly. You can't even say it. Poison. Here, we can still choose to see nothing. Here we're sheltered for the moment. Maybe. But this is one of my bad days.

ZOE *falls silent.* RICHARD *is more and more anguished.* PAZ *washes her pistols with conviction.*

8.

On a park bench.

ARTAUD has a little bottle of laudanum in his hands. He takes several drops from it with a dropper and offers it to RENÉ.

ARTAUD   Laudanum?

RENÉ opens his mouth. ARTAUD squeezes a few drops of laudanum onto his tongue.

RENÉ   Thank you.

They settle onto the bench, happy, drugged, speaking with joyous indifference.

All the same: that Anaïs... what a slut.

ARTAUD   An unscrupulous slut who sucks vital energy and diffuses it. Diffuses it...

RENÉ   Did you see how she broke away from us both? As if we'd never done anything for her, whereas everyone knows it's thanks to men like us—open-minded, liberal—that her intellect has been able to bloom.

ARTAUD   Some women are like that. Even with a multitude of open doors in front of them, they always pick the same one. The door of pleasure and ingratitude. It's their way of being free.

RENÉ   Oh, I always knew she was a slut. I sound as if I were surprised, but I am not surprised.

         ARTAUD *takes a few drops of laudanum, offers some to* RENÉ, *who accepts.*

ARTAUD   They love men so much they end up swallowing them whole. They're not in love: they're hungry.

RENÉ   The truth is, she's dangerous.

ARTAUD   Women like Anaïs suffer from a mysterious disease. Obsessed with pleasure, just as a plague victim is riddled with the plague, and secretly wishing to infect everyone else.

RENÉ   She wanted to infect me, too. As soon as she set foot in my office. She tried everything to seduce me. Then to emasculate me. The bitch.

ARTAUD   Unssssscrupulousssss slutsssss.

RENÉ   At first, I didn't suspect a thing. Such a delicate woman. Perverse. It was perfect. But it was a ruse.

ARTAUD   So many people want to subject others to false pleasure. But in false pleasure, after a while, there remains only the falseness. Danger is everywhere. Yet I'm the one they put in isolation, I'm the one they lock up.

RENÉ   She pleasured me. I thought, she's giving herself to me. But no, she was just taking a holiday on my body. She used me.

ARTAUD   They need to be locked up, male, female, all of them. With their contaminant abyss.

RENÉ   Absolutely.

            They help themselves to more laudanum, generously.

ARTAUD   There is a certain race of people who block knowledge and truth. Prisoners of their sex.

RENÉ   It was her sex that got me, no doubt about it.

ARTAUD   Lock them up before they reduce us all to something—

RENÉ   —Something soft.

ARTAUD   Exhibitionists, constantly climaxing and polluting the purity of the global soul.

RENÉ   Let's go talk to her, Artaud. Let's go find her at the café.

They are truly in an altered state.

ARTAUD   The cafés must be emptied of all who are obsessed with pleasure.

RENÉ   Yes, we'll go find her at the café and then put her in a room somewhere. In the country.

ARTAUD   Lock them away in a tower with closed windows.

RENÉ   We'll put Anaïs in isolation, in quarantine.

ARTAUD   And the years will go by...

RENÉ   Over the years, her slut libido will drift off to sleep. She'll return to a more classic love of things and of men.

ARTAUD   To stop the alienating surface of things from growing so thick that the profound, hidden by rocky layers of aesthetic flash, becomes unattainable.

RENÉ   We must save her, Artaud. Save her from herself before she becomes vulgar.

ARTAUD   Save the spermatic profundity of the decadent human race.

           They take more laudanum, this time by the spoonful.

RENÉ   Let's go to the café, Artaud.

ARTAUD   Yes, let's go to the café. To fight the plague victims, swilling their bottles of red.

RENÉ   We must rescue Anaïs from the tower.

ARTAUD   Rescue Anaïs?

RENÉ   I love her.

ARTAUD   You're sick. I don't want to listen to you.

RENÉ   Anaïs is trapped in a tower and only we can save her. I want to save her. And she will finally love me.

ARTAUD   You're infected. Be quiet.

           ARTAUD *impatiently takes another spoonful of laudanum.*

RENÉ   *(panicked, sad)* She's never loved me, really.

ARTAUD   You whine like a child. It's repugnant.

                ARTAUD *puts his hands over his ears, childishly.*

RENÉ   But if we save her, she'll love me.

                ARTAUD *starts reciting loudly to drown out* RENÉ*'s words.*

ARTAUD   Saturation
                Exposure
                Howl

RENÉ   I'm skinny and emasculated—

ARTAUD   *(reciting)* —Saturation
                Exposure
                Howl
                Saturated
                Desire
                Saturated

RENÉ   I hate her but she's stronger than me, so I love her.

ARTAUD   *(interrupts him, shouting)* Will you please shut up!
                Saturation
                Exposure
                Howl
                Saturated

Desire
Saturated
World
Saturated

RENÉ   I want to crawl back to her—

ARTAUD   —Liberty
Dead
Quest
Saturated
Head
Head
Head
Hole
Saturation
Decapitated
By your
Diseased
Hurtful
Hands
I want to be sublime
Liberty
Dead
Head
Head
Head
Hole
Hurtful
I want to be sublime

Pause. ARTAUD *leaves.*

RENÉ   Completely emasculated.

            Noticing that ARTAUD *is gone, he goes off in search of him.*

            Artaud? What are you doing? I need you. I'm emasculated, Artaud. Artaud!

9.

In the café.

PAZ and RICHARD eat cold cuts and drink red wine.

ANAÏS writes in her journal, off to one side, discreetly. ZOE is motionless.

PAZ   I'd love to fight, but not at the front. That's just ridiculous. Killing people at random. Whoops, a German, whoops, a Russian.

RICHARD   And beneath it all, they might have been decent blokes.

PAZ   That's what I'm saying... It's random.

RICHARD   Killing people at random accomplishes nothing.

PAZ   You have to kill the right people... Not the soldier messing his pants and wanting to die. No. So: who do you assassinate?

RICHARD   An artist. Kill an artist. Protesters by the thousands will take to the streets.

PAZ   Nah.

RICHARD   We'd carry his corpse above our heads. Women would weep. Men would want to fight… And they'd want freedom. When an artist is murdered we all want freedom. Because we've lost everything that the artist hasn't had time to create. We've lost the solution he would have thought of. Kill an artist.

PAZ   I hate artists. They'll make him a martyr. That'll be worse…

ANAÏS   You ought to kill a woman.

RICHARD   *(laughing)* A woman!

PAZ   Might as well kill a child. What impact will that have? It's pointless to kill a woman. It's a sacrifice that means nothing.

ANAÏS   Depends on the woman…

RICHARD   We keep coming back to the same problem: whom do you assassinate?

PAZ   The more important the person you kill, the fewer people you need to kill. It's only logical. A woman? I don't think so. An artist? No. It has to be a man with power.

RICHARD   *(checking the time)* Well, I'm going to go stretch my legs.

PAZ   Already?

ZOE   Three o'clock.

> RICHARD *hasn't managed to leave before he is struck by* ZOE's *words. He is rooted to the spot with anguish.* PAZ *pours a glass of port and serves it to* ZOE, *who drinks it and places the empty glass next to the others. There are now four glasses on the table.*

This morning while scrubbing a toilet bowl, I had a vision… America. Children running in a park. Skyscrapers, flags. People cooking sausages. It's a holiday. But something goes wrong. There's a storm and everyone runs for cover as if it was the end of the world. As if the rain wasn't rain but something else. There's a tall blonde so tipsy she's stumbling around, and no one's coming to take her home. She collapses in the merciless rain.

> *Pause.*

America the Blonde will rule for a while. America the Blonde will stumble around. She'll remake everything. Why, she'll even try to remake us. To say that "Paris in the thirties was such-and-such... Before the Second War. Before the horror... They were already dreaming of the American Dream... without knowing it..." It will be the revenge of the bastard child. But there's something that will elude America for a long, long time: the truth. She's too much built on dreams to love the truth. Like June.

JUNE enters the café, followed by GERMAIN.

Hello, June, the American.

JUNE and ANAÏS see each other.

ANAÏS   *(rising)* June!

JUNE   Anaïs.

> *The lighting changes. The café disappears for a second: only the two of them remain. Then the café reappears and they both have vanished. ANAÏS has left her journal behind.*

GERMAIN   June? June!

10.

In the street.

FRED *finds* LATIMBRÉE. *She is sitting, and singing, not very well.*

FRED I have your two hundred francs.

He presents her with the two hundred francs. She signals him to be quiet and finishes her song on a sharp, unpleasant note. FRED *is impatient.*

Well, if you don't want to anymore, we'll just forget about it.

She takes and counts the two hundred francs.

LATIMBRÉE Come. You're treating yourself to the very best. You're going to love it. Relax.

FRED I'll relax when I've tasted the merchandise.

LATIMBRÉE   Certainly. Shall I start by whipping off my skirt, or
            a poem?

FRED   Let's do the sk—

LATIMBRÉE   *(interrupting)* Here: I'm so soft-hearted I'll throw in
            a prologue for free.

> FRED *is getting impatient.*

> "Poem for the Hole in the World."

> In the world there is a hole
> Large as the leprosy of lepers
> And in this hole as bare as desert
> Diseased deserters
> Hide edible treasures...

FRED   It's... it's not very good.

LATIMBRÉE   Clearly, I don't find you hugely inspiring.

FRED   Well then, I'll just take back my two hundred francs.

LATIMBRÉE   Now, now. We should be all right, so long as you
            mount me from behind.

> *She disappears behind a tree or a building.*

FRED   *(happily)* Good: let's get down to business.

He follows her. We see only the top half of
LATIMBRÉE, *who is receiving the thrusts of* FRED.

LATIMBRÉE   When astride the earth
Storms and scourges
Tighten their thighs
The earth pinched gallops off into the dark
And men like ants
Seized with raw-boned panic
Hurl themselves on each other
In mutual slaughter
As their instincts have promised
For worlds and for ages
These luckless men
With limp hearts and firm sexes
Will find they are a sacrifice
To all these female thunderbolts

RENÉ *arrives, still high, and, seeing* LATIMBRÉE, *is*
struck by her bizarre posture.

And as the sky lights up
The landscape, exposed guts
And ripped-open men
Raw and overflowing with blood
Will form the backdrop of life—

He goes toward her, interrupting.

RENÉ —Pardon me, you didn't happen to see a man go by with rather lunatic eyes and… complicated hair. A somewhat flamboyant man—

FRED *(poking his head around the corner)* —What's going on?

LATIMBRÉE *(to FRED)* He's lost.

RENÉ I'm looking for—

FRED —Can't you see we're busy?

> RENÉ *looks at them, confused.*

RENÉ Of course. You're right. I hadn't noticed.

FRED Move along! Nothing to see here!

> RENÉ *looks at* FRED, *offended, then turns to* LATIMBRÉE.

RENÉ I'm looking for a woman too—

FRED —Get your sorry face out of here.

RENÉ Yes, good. Thanks anyway.

> RENÉ *goes a little ways away and sits down, staring vacantly.*

LATIMBRÉE   Is that it? Are we done?

FRED   No.

LATIMBRÉE   You're all soft.

FRED   Let's pick up where we left off…

LATIMBRÉE   *(with diminished enthusiasm)* And as the sky lights up
The landscape, exposed guts—

FRED   —That's it. That's it.

LATIMBRÉE   And ripped-open men
Raw and overflowing with blood
Will form the backdrop of life—

> RENÉ *hallucinates. A clarinet descends from
> the sky beside him, as if his hallucination were
> becoming real. Wonderstruck, he plays the instru-
> ment.* LATIMBRÉE, *disturbed by the music, stops
> reciting her poem.* FRED *keeps going.*

FRED   Yes, yes, that's good.

LATIMBRÉE   Stop! Stop, it's over. I can't. He stifles my inspiration.

FRED   *(continuing)* Almost done—

> *She slips out of* FRED's *grasp.*

LATIMBRÉE   —No, I've finished… I don't like being interrupted.

FRED   *(trying to get her back)* Me neither.

LATIMBRÉE   Too bad.

>   *She manages to get away from* FRED.

>   And I'm keeping the two hundred francs.

FRED   What about me?

LATIMBRÉE   I don't care. I can't teach you everything.

>   FRED *is surprised at his own state, short of breath.*

FRED   I don't know what I'm going to do. I feel sort of… crazy. Dangerous.

LATIMBRÉE   Like a beast that has tasted human flesh; I warned you.

>   *LATIMBRÉE leaves.*

FRED   Shit! Shit!

>   RENÉ *finishes his blues, very inspired.* FRED *approaches him, assaults him, rifles through his pockets.*

11.

At the café, in the restroom.

JUNE and ANAÏS circle each other, touching each other's hair and arms, staring intensely.

ANAÏS   You are always so perfectly brutal and sensual.

JUNE   I love the way you dress! So classy... Almost nothing's showing, except your neck.

ANAÏS   For the first time in so long, I feel that I exist.

JUNE   *(taking ANAÏS's hand)* I love your hands. Remember that, huh, how I'd look at your hands?

ANAÏS   You repeat old gestures and it's as if everything were still possible. As if time could do nothing against us.

JUNE   I want to be with you again. I can't tell you everything, where I've been, what I've been doing over the

years. I don't want to know who you've turned into.
I just want to be with you again.

ANAÏS   I'm here. I'm real with you, I'm myself...

There is a knock at the door.

JUNE   Someone's there!

GERMAIN   It's me, June. It's Germain. What the hell are you
             doing? Come out of there.

JUNE   Knock it off, okay.

ANAÏS   Germain? Who is that?

JUNE   I happened to run into him this morning.

ANAÏS   You're lying. You spent the whole night drinking
             together.

JUNE   Okay, so I drank. All night. I was goddamn jumpy
             about seeing you again. Jealous, Anaïs?

ANAÏS   *(fascinated)* Yes. Tell me.

JUNE lights a cigarette, smokes.

*She is hesitant, making up her story as she goes
along.*

JUNE   I spent the night in a gloomy joint… where the men
                were drinking and talking too loud. I was the only
                woman, I was alone… At my table, I could feel men's
                eyes all over me. I wanted to throw myself at them,
                or scream… or scram. It was scary in there, and it
                was sexy as hell.

                ANAÏS slides to JUNE's feet, caressing her legs.

ANAÏS   I wish I had been there. I wish I had been you. To
                give myself to the point of drowning…

JUNE   Slowly, I let the strap of my dress slide down my
                shoulder. I uncovered one breast… The men were
                devouring me with their eyes. And right there in
                front of all of them, I started stroking my breast.
                The men watching me, you coulda heard a pin drop
                they were so excited. So much pleasure I drowned
                in it.

ANAÏS   Let us be drowned. That's so lovely, so lovely. I love
                you, June.

                More knocking.

GERMAIN   June?

JUNE   *(putting her finger to ANAÏS's lips)* Shhhhhhhhh.

GERMAIN   June? Answer me.

ANAÏS   Let's get out of here.

               *JUNE looks at herself in the mirror. Her makeup is
               smeared. Her stockings are torn.*

JUNE   I'm a wreck...

               ANAÏS takes a pair of silk stockings out of her purse.

ANAÏS   Take them...

               JUNE puts the stockings on.

JUNE   Wish I was like you. So delicate. So feminine.

ANAÏS   No. You. You are perfect. Here.

               *ANAÏS holds lipstick out to JUNE, but JUNE doesn't
               take it. Instead, she takes ANAÏS's hand.*

JUNE   No, you. Draw the lipstick onto my mouth.

ANAÏS   *(uneasy)* But I—

               *JUNE takes ANAÏS's hand and guides it to her lips.
               ANAÏS applies the lipstick.*

JUNE   Anaïs, I wanna kiss you.

ANAÏS   Yes, June, I want to kiss you.

A long kiss. JUNE *takes* ANAÏS *by the hand and leads her toward the exit. There is a knocking at the door.*

JUNE   C'mon.

They leave by the window.

12.

At the café.

*GERMAIN is sitting up against the washroom door.
ZOE is checking the time. PAZ is cleaning glasses
and pistols.*

GERMAIN   I did it again. I got plastered and I believed it. I really
believed I would become someone else... That I'd
find myself and escape myself at the same time. That
I was on the scent.

PAZ   A real hunter.

GERMAIN   A hunter who tracks himself. Like a cat chasing its
own tail.

PAZ   *(half-sincere, half-mocking)* Cats do catch their tails,
sometimes. Doesn't do any good, but they catch
them anyway.

GERMAIN   I hunt but I never find. I don't know who I am. I
            never catch. I'd like to've been a Dame Pipi, like the
            old lady. I'd like to've been an ancient prophet since
            birth. To say "the sky will darken" and watch the sky
            darken. But no, I'm still just killing time.

PAZ   Everyone's killing time. Not just you.

GERMAIN   I wish I was June. I wish I was America and sensu-
            ality. Or a banker. A miser. If I was a miser, I'd live
            for my money. At least I'd know why I'm alive. But
            the truth is, I couldn't care less about money. Bring
            me a glass, Paz. I'll give you all my money.

            *PAZ serves him, singing. GERMAIN lets himself be
            tempted, goes to the piano, and sings with her.
            They are interrupted by ZOE.*

ZOE   Six p.m.

            *PAZ serves a glass of port to ZOE, who drinks it
            immediately. There are now seven empty glasses
            in front of ZOE.*

            Everyone's dallying, rolling around on top of each
            other like they're searching for something to hold on
            to. And yet we're surprised to see huge crowds follow-
            ing Stalin, Hitler, Mussolini, or Franco. And we'll be
            surprised when ordinary people commit atrocities.
            We'll say, "How could they have gone that far?"

She gets up.

But come on. What about you? You think you wouldn't do exactly the same as everyone else? You think you're not capable of atrocities?

She sits back down.

With all the massacres on their way, how do you know which of you will be massacred and who will do the massacring?

Pause. She laughs.

LATIMBRÉE *enters the café.*

LATIMBRÉE I have the loveliest ankles in Paris and I am unbelievably thirsty.

ZOE Between the sixth and seventh glass of port, I always have the same desire to go for a stroll in an English garden—

LATIMBRÉE *(interrupting* ZOE*)* —I'll have champagne and olives. I always drink my champagne with olives. It's because of the bubbles. I like putting things of the same shape together. Don't you find that about bubbles in champagne: without olives, you can't appreciate how little they are?

ZOE English gardens pretend to imitate nature. And that's
absurd when you think about it. Why imitate nature?
You don't have to do anything to nature: all it wants
is to be. Soon, leisure and spectacle will take up
so much space, representation will invade imagination to the point that man will try to imitate himself
rather than live. Man will become his own English
garden. After the massacres, that is. Maybe it's a form
of self-defence. To seek out that thing you see in the
eyes of man and beast, in the blossoms of trees, in
the fruit of the land. Scorched by the horror but not
yet dead.

> ZOE *falls silent, having said her piece. Silence.*
> *Unease.* LATIMBRÉE, *to overcome the silence, starts*
> *telling a story.*

LATIMBRÉE I slept with Stalin last week.

> PAZ *arrives with champagne and olives.*

PAZ Stalin?

LATIMBRÉE Yes, yes, Stalin. Well I almost slept with Stalin. I'm
walking the streets and a Russian comes by. He tells
me to follow him, in Russian and in mime. He smells
of vodka and hay, but I don't make fun. I never judge
my clients. You mustn't. He takes me to the Hotel de
la Paix… that shabby, seedy one. Stalin at the Hotel
de la Paix! Just thinking of it, I can't help myself, I

burst out laughing. The Russian doesn't understand. So I laugh alone. No matter, I'm used to it.

PAZ   ` And Stalin was in the room? Stalin, the real one?

LATIMBRÉE   I get to the hotel. I go up to the second floor. Halfway up the stairs he signals me to wait. He goes to the door, knocks three times, like a code. He goes into the room. I wait. I get restless. When he comes back, I tell him, "Took you long enough." He signals me to be quiet and takes me by the arm so I'll go up.

PAZ   And then he was there, in the room.

LATIMBRÉE   We get to the door! Again he knocks three times. Same code. Someone lets us in. In the room there are five Russians. Only one of them is wearing a moustache, that's Stalin. He's sitting at a little empty table, and you know what he's working on? A house of cards. So we wait. Nobody moves. The four Russians watch Stalin build his house of cards. And between you and me, I'm thinking: so what if it *is* Stalin sitting there, making a stupid little house of cards? I mean, *really!* Eight times the cards fall down and he starts over again, and it goes on for ages.

GERMAIN   What then?

LATIMBRÉE   Then, finally, he manages to make his house stand up. So the Russians are all happy for good old Stalin;

they start clapping, and with all the commotion, the house of cards falls down... and Stalin puts his moustache back on and says: *"Chert voz'mi."**

PAZ　　　　　It wasn't Stalin.

LATIMBRÉE　It was Stalin. After that they brought me over to him and he prodded me all over like I was a piglet, and when he saw I had a nice bum, he said, *"Horosho."*†

PAZ　　　　　And you slept with him?

LATIMBRÉE　I told him two hundred francs.

GERMAIN　　You asked Stalin for two hundred francs?

LATIMBRÉE　Absolutely: I'm no communist. Anyway, I've never done it without being paid: doing it for pleasure is a sin. I didn't make the rules.

GERMAIN　　She's making it up! Stalin at the old Hotel de la Paix! Honestly.

PAZ　　　　　So what happened?

LATIMBRÉE　Nothing. Those rotten Russians, they only had rubles. Can you believe it? No one in that bloody

---

* Russian: "The Devil take it."

† Russian: "Good."

room had francs. That just goes to show you how
much money there is in communism.

PAZ   And then?

LATIMBRÉE   I left.

GERMAIN   They let you go? A roomful of Russians, including
Stalin himself, who you refuse to screw because he
hasn't got two hundred francs, and you get out alive.

LATIMBRÉE   Absolutely. I know how to have cordial relations with
people.

GERMAIN   And that's how it ends, with Stalin telling you, "Sorry,
next time I'll have francs."

LATIMBRÉE   Stalin didn't say anything and I left. But first I warned
the hotel-keeper his guests were broke. I considered
it my civic duty.

PAZ   You should have gunned him down.

GERMAIN   Gun down Stalin? Why? What has Stalin ever done
to you—

PAZ   —When you're so poor you might as well not exist,
when you're no more than an insect in a great sea
of insects, and you find yourself standing in front of
Stalin, you gun him down. You don't ask questions,

you take a pistol and fire. That's why pistols were
invented: so everyone would be equal.

LATIMBRÉE Well off you go, then. Good old Hotel de la Paix,
second floor. Three little knocks. And there you are.
You shoot, and that's the end of that. Great men! I've
known tons of them. Did you know it was the great
Houdini himself who deflowered me?

Music.

13.

In a brothel.

Intense music. JUNE *and* ANAÏS *are drinking together in a little booth surrounded by mirrors.*

ANAÏS   I love coming to brothels. Seeing all these men and women buzzing around money.

JUNE   Money is sexy when you talk about it. Because you're always really talking about something else.

             ANAÏS *takes out her billfold.*

ANAÏS   I'm much less wealthy than I was, you know.

JUNE   So, even more of a kick to blow your cash.

             They laugh. JUNE *holds her cigarette to* ANAÏS's *lips so she can take a drag.*

ANAÏS   Let's buy a drink for that young girl over there.

JUNE   That blonde? I don't think so.

ANAÏS   I like her, June—she looks like you. These women fascinate me. Imagine all the things they know. They have known every kind of man.

JUNE   And that's why they don't know anything about them. *Men* get lost inside tired old clichés. Little ones. Big ones. Smelly ones. Not-so-smelly ones. It all gets so boring. Gimme a kiss, Anaïs.

ANAÏS   Look at the little one with the black hair. She could be my sister.

JUNE   What are you up to, Anaïs, huh? It's like you're looking through them trying to see us.

ANAÏS   They fascinate me.

JUNE   You get a thrill out of pretending you have no choice, pretending you've gotta screw for cash.

ANAÏS   I would be detached from my own body, absent, ultimately hiding somewhere else.

JUNE   You always romanticise. You did the same thing with me. You project your fantasies onto other women, especially really poor women, instead of seeing them as they are.

ANAÏS   You're right about them, June, it's true. But not about
          you, not now. I see you as you are and I am still in
          love with you.

          They kiss, for a long time. JUNE breaks it off
          sharply.

JUNE   Anaïs, let's be ladies of the evening too.

ANAÏS   What?

JUNE   Let's get undressed and join the girls. I want a man
          to pay you. A man you don't choose.

ANAÏS   No. I prefer to stay on this side of the erotic line and
          to spend all my money with you, on you.

JUNE   We've played that damn scene to death already.
          C'mon, follow me. Go on, Anaïs.

ANAÏS   No, I don't want to. It's not me.

JUNE   Oh yes it is. Whaddaya think? Think you're so dif-
          ferent from them? So different from me?

ANAÏS   I'm not the kind of woman who doesn't choose.

JUNE   So you and me, Anaïs, we're not the same breed, is
          that it?

ANAÏS   Of course we are… We're sisters, lovers.

JUNE   No: I'm the kind of woman who doesn't choose. Always have been. And that's why you love me so goddamn much. You project yourself into me, you get your kicks through me. And afterwards you slip back into your comfy little doll slippers—

ANAÏS   —Stop. Don't be that way.

JUNE   When I act the whore, I don't watch myself acting the whore, I act the whore. When I live, I live. Every day, I could ruin my whole life, forever… I don't get another shot through fiction. I can't reinvent myself in words. You and all the rest of them… painters, writers, whatever… You come and you climb down into our little hell and you play at being like us. In the name of art you come and stir our shit, and you're so filled with wonder you lead us into even deeper shit, because our shit is so goddamned appealing. Then you leave us to our fate, without protection, without art. You leave us so you can go paint, or write! Literature! What a load of hooey.

ANAÏS   I will protect you—

JUNE   —Go and get a client!

ANAÏS   No.

JUNE   Come on, Anaïs, we all know the biggest slut in this joint is you.

ANAÏS   No.

              ANAÏS *gets up, covers herself, prepares to leave.*

              I'm the kind of woman who chooses. I've even chosen to be the kind of woman who chooses. Not a slut. Free. That's all.

              ANAÏS *goes.* JUNE *drinks.*

14.

In the café.

LATIMBRÉE sings. PAZ, downstage, is loading a pistol. RICHARD arrives behind her.

RICHARD   *(tickling PAZ, awkwardly)* Yoohoo, it's me!

PAZ quickly hides her pistol and looks hard at RICHARD, but he is already looking elsewhere, upset by LATIMBRÉE's song.

What's going on?

PAZ   What?

RICHARD   There, at the piano. What's she doing?

PAZ   Singing, what do you think!

RICHARD   But… she's singing my poems!

PAZ   Oh, save me.

RICHARD   You recognise my style, at least? Those poems
           are mine!

           Unable to breathe.

           Perhaps I'm translucent or, no, perhaps my mind
           vibrates so strongly that everyone can tune into my
           ideas without my knowing it…

PAZ   (*sighing*) Richard, I'm begging you! I don't have time
           for your stories. Not now…

RICHARD   Paz: I'm going to throw myself in the Seine.

PAZ   Here we go again.

RICHARD   Don't try to stop me. It's too late, I'm going to throw
           myself in the Seine.

PAZ   All right, goodbye!

           She goes.

RENÉ   Richard, Richard, Richard… You know why I'm cer-
           tain that I didn't steal your novel? Because I don't
           listen to you when you talk. Normally, I listen to all
           of my patients with intense attention and nothing
           escapes me, not one detail. But with you, it's not the

same. I don't know why, but I cannot maintain my concentration. Perhaps it's the way you formulate your sentences… Quite simply, you hypnotise me, Richard. And after a while, I don't hear a thing. So you can rest assured, I did not steal your novel.

He takes him by the shoulders, in a friendly manner.

Feel better now?

RICHARD   It doesn't matter anymore. I'm going to throw myself in the Seine.

RENÉ doesn't react. Pause. RICHARD waits.

René?

RENÉ   Yes?

RENÉ understands what has just happened, and finds it very funny.

Oh, you see? It happened again! You were talking and I wasn't listening. It's as if I never even heard you. Amazing.

RICHARD   *(emphasising each word)* I'm going to throw myself in the Seine.

RENÉ   *(who has been listening attentively, nodding)* Why
              not? Normally I would offer you platitudes along
              the lines of: "Don't talk that way. You're better than
              that." But when you get right down to it, why bother?
              I tell you, Richard, if that's what you want… Why
              not? Why not!

              RICHARD, *depressed, goes to sit down, near* GERMAIN.

              RENÉ *hums to himself, finding a tune he likes,
              and starts to dance.*

              Why not! Why not? Why not! Why not? Why not!

              ARTAUD *arrives.*

              (getting hold of himself) Artaud! There you are. I've
              been looking for you everywhere.

ARTAUD   Please. Leave my table.

RENÉ   What's gotten into you?

ARTAUD   I am very very busy.

RENÉ   Surely you have a bit of time for your old friend.

ARTAUD   I don't understand what you are referring to when you
              say the word "friend." It doesn't exist for me. Not today.

RENÉ   Come off it, Tony!

> RENÉ, *still under the effect of the drug, jostles him
> much too familiarly.* ARTAUD *looks daggers at him.*

All right. I understand… But… you wouldn't happen
to have a bit of… of… you know, the laudanum you
shared with me, a while ago…

> *Pause.*

Fine, all right, I understand…

> RENÉ *leaves* ARTAUD's *table.* LATIMBRÉE *sees* ARTAUD
> *from afar and comes out from behind the piano.*

LATIMBRÉE   Look, it's darling Artaud! Hi there, Artaud.

ARTAUD   Please…

> LATIMBRÉE *begins to sing.*

Let me work!

> *She continues to sing.*

Silence, I beg you.

> FRED *finds* ANAÏS's *journal and reads it.* RICHARD
> *comes over.*

RICHARD   Fred. Nice knowing you. I'm going to throw myself in the Seine.

> *FRED pays no attention and keeps reading. RICHARD wanders around the café. JUNE enters and sits at the piano with GERMAIN.*

JUNE   *(to GERMAIN)* I thought I came back to Paris to find Anaïs, but it's not for nothing I found you first. 'Cause you and me, we're from the class that doesn't choose. We mooch around, restless, looking for someone to shine us up and treat us like gods. We're not enough on our own. We're like a graph with no axis…

> *Pause.*

If I turned my back on madness, right here, tonight, I could change my fate. But I'm not that kind of woman. I'm going to drift into madness and stay there, like a slave.

> *Louder.*

I've got no power. Just charm. Useless goddamn charm.

> *RICHARD comes over to GERMAIN and JUNE.*

RICHARD   Hello, I'm Richard.

GERMAIN   Germain.

JUNE   June.

RICHARD   June, Germain, pleased to meet you. I'm going to throw myself in the Seine.

JUNE   You don't say?

RICHARD   You see that bridge over there, I'm going to throw myself off that bridge.

GERMAIN   Which bridge?

RICHARD   That one. Right there. See, there's a fellow crossing it.

GERMAIN   But that's just a little bridge. You think it's high enough?

            They look.

RICHARD   Of course it's high enough!

GERMAIN   Don't think so, no… you'd be wasting your time there.

RICHARD   It's high enough, I tell you!

GERMAIN   No… Don't think so—

JUNE   —You gotta be kidding me! Did you see that?

RICHARD   *(who hasn't seen)* What? What happened?

GERMAIN   Unbelievable.

JUNE   That guy crossing the bridge! He just threw himself
                in the Seine.

RICHARD   Copycat! Another copycat. I'm losing my mind.

                PAZ enters and crosses to RICHARD.

PAZ   Richard? Richard, come here, I need you.

RICHARD   I'm done for, Paz… Incapable of living. Incapable of
                dying. Done for.

PAZ   No. Pull yourself together—

RICHARD   —What's the point.

                *PAZ shouts at RICHARD, perhaps even physically
                shaking him.*

PAZ   Dammit, Richard! Pull yourself together and listen
                to me.

                RICHARD, startled, listens to PAZ.

I've always wanted to do something important. Always felt I was meant for more than serving glasses, washing glasses, scrubbing glasses... The violence I feel is not in vain. It's leading me somewhere. With the hands of a glass-washer, with the rage of a helpless female, with my rebellion, my bone-deep rebellion, I'm going to change history. And you will be my witness. You're going to make me a painting.

RICHARD   Can't. Don't know how. I'm not a witness.

PAZ   I will describe it to you in detail and you will paint it. You will stop whining and do what I tell you. You will be an artist, for real. For once.

RICHARD   All right. I'll do it. For you.

Already proud, already too carried away.

I'll paint your painting!

They go out.

ZOE   Nine o'clock.

Time to lighten the mood. Let me tell you the story of a child who is having a tantrum. She breaks a bottle and cuts her fingers. Her fingers bleed. How awful. She's afraid she's going to drip everywhere, stain everything, and die. She drips. She stains everything.

But she doesn't die. So now she has to live with her own blood on her own sweater, which is worse than dying. Now that she knows she can be stained and the stain can come from her, all she can do is get herself more stained. Once you're stained, that's all you can do. In the end, you accept the stain, and live.

    Pause.

Live.

    Pause.

    In the café, festive music and songs. LATIMBRÉE *dances.*

    ANAÏS *enters and looks for her notebook.* RENÉ *sees her and comes toward her.*

RENÉ   Anaïsssss? I've been looking for you. I'm going to save you. You're trapped in a tower of sluts. It's not your fault. And I'm going to save you.

ANAÏS   To save me! Well go right ahead, dear. I've been waiting for you.

    RENÉ *makes a move toward her, attempts to take her in his arms as a knight would a princess. It does not go well.*

RENÉ   Not today.

ANAÏS   I thought as much.

RENÉ   I'm too inebriated. Tomorrow. I'll save you tomorrow!
            Right now, I'm enjoying inebriation. Don't feel like
            saving anybody.

ANAÏS   You didn't happen to see my notebook?

RENÉ   *(not listening)* Perhaps not tomorrow either... You
            never know with inebriation. It might last!

ANAÏS   René! My notebook!

RENÉ   Notebook?

ANAÏS   I'm looking for my notebook. I was writing; I left, my
            mind was elsewhere, and I left my notebook.

RENÉ   You left your diary?

ANAÏS   My mind was elsewhere.

RENÉ   Then I shall help you. Right. Right. Right. A note-
            book. A notebook. A notebook.

            *He starts looking but soon forgets what he was
            doing. Too far gone, he hums, in a rhythm of his
            own, very bluesy.*

A notebook… Looking, looking, looking, for a notebook…

RENÉ drifts away from ANAÏS. LATIMBRÉE, dancing and singing, motions to RENÉ to come and join her.

Enter ARTAUD.

ARTAUD   Silence!

Everyone stops.

This.
All of this.
Is.
All of this is a play.

He is on fire.

The plague is a play. The plague once established in a city destroys the institutions of that city. Chaos takes hold. Funeral pyres ignite to burn the bodies of the diseased.
Everyone wants a pyre.
Here, in this café, a pyre.
Here, in this play, a pyre.
Here, on these boards, plague-ridden corpses.

He looks at the actors. Pause. More calmly.

The plague is a play wherein recovered victims transform themselves, seized with the need to be the opposite of what they had been. The chaste turn lascivious, the lascivious turn pure. Attainted, they throw themselves into lust or horror: indestructible, empty.
Happy and empty.

Pause. He continues suddenly, more fiercely.

The plague is a play.
Here, on these boards, plague-ridden corpses.

He looks at the actors. Pause.

Plague-ridden corpses are like actors. They give themselves over, unconscious, terrorised. The bodies are intact but ravaged by a foreign illness, transfixed by emotions that belong to no one. Emotions that have no ties except with reality. Emotions that wish to be reality.
A play is like the plague in that it acts and avenges. It liquidates reality even as it submits to it. Exposing latent sadism and cruelty. Revealing the perverse pathways of the spirit.
This is a play.
This is a play and even as the plague explodes and as this play explodes so that perverse reality may triumph over the institutional banking constructions

of our cities and strongholds, the plague victims and
the actors, with one breath, cry out for rebellion.
This, now, me, us, is the contagion.
The epidemic.

15.

In the background ANAÏS *is still looking for her
notebook.*

FRED   What are you looking for?

ANAÏS   Give it.

FRED   Oh, I'll give it to you. Don't you worry about that.

        He forces her into the washroom, discreetly.

ANAÏS   *(laughing, surprised)* What's gotten into you? Cut
        it out.

FRED   Shut up.

ANAÏS   You don't get to decide to help yourself. You don't
        get to decide whether I screw you or not.

FRED   Oh no?

ANAÏS   Don't be stupid. Are you actually going to force your-
               self on me?

FRED   *(laughs)* I feel like having a girl who doesn't want to.

ANAÏS   You're ridiculous. Let me go.

               *He crushes her against him, grabs her breasts.
               Tears her dress. ANAÏS fends him off, but he's stron-
               ger than she is and manages to overpower her.
               ANAÏS fights him, cries out. FRED hurts her. While
               he is taking her from behind by force, ANAÏS lifts
               her head, furious, dignified.*

               (icy) I can find the strength inside myself to stop you
               ripping away any part of me, to make sure you take
               nothing that is mine. You will not rob me of the
               tiniest part of pleasure. Rape me? Me?

FRED   Shut up!

ANAÏS   Moron. I'm the one who decides. I have transformed
               pain, I have freed myself from any role of victim that
               might have been mine. Rape me? Impossible. All
               pleasures are possible and all pleasures are mine. I
               have demolished all taboos precisely so that I will
               never be a victim. I am unrapable. Do what you
               want. It changes nothing.

FRED *climaxes, but* ANAÏS *buries his sighs of plea-sure with her cries.*

The pleasure is mine!
Mine!
Mine!

He lets her fall to the ground, throws her notebook on her back, and leaves the washroom.

Mine.

ANAÏS *punches a cupboard, enraged. This causes a small mirror to fall and break. Behind the mirror is a pistol. Someone had hidden a pistol there.*

ANAÏS *takes the pistol.*

The music from the café continues even more strongly. Louder. Livelier.

16.

In the café.

JUNE is singing, GERMAIN is at the piano. They are finishing a blues number.

JUNE Paris jerks sideways beneath my feet and I crash onto the pavement. Everything disappears, Germain. My kisses mean squat. I could give 'em to everyone. They're empty. Want me to kiss you?

GERMAIN No. Hold onto your mouth. Hold onto yourself. You're so lovely. So pure.

JUNE I'm a shadow. A shadow, and lost.

GERMAIN I'm here. I'm not going anywhere... I'm here now and I'm staying... June?

JUNE *(not listening to him)* I'm a whole bunch of Junes. Hazy. Hazy.

RICHARD *enters, in a panic, profoundly unsettled.*

RICHARD   Paz! Paz! You have to take your painting back. I can't do it. Paz?

FRED, *not* PAZ, *is washing glasses.*

(to FRED*)* What are you doing there?

FRED   What's it look like?

RICHARD   You're washing glasses!

FRED   I'm washing glasses.

RICHARD   Why?

FRED   Because. I dunno.

RICHARD   But you can't. It's always Paz there doing the dishes. You have no right to do the dishes. Paz?

RICHARD *looks for* PAZ, *without success.* FRED *continues washing glasses.*

(to the absent PAZ*)* Take your painting back, Paz! I give up. I can't do your painting. You can't ask that of me…
She said,
"Paint the night, with the lights bursting out of it.

The café, white on black background. Walls. Tables.
Paint my brother washing glasses for once.
Paint Zoe with nothing to drink.
Germain who is unhappy.
Not Anaïs, though. Even if you see her, even if she's
there in your head. You mustn't paint Anaïs. Because
I don't understand her."
She said, "Paint the American with the madness in
her eyes.
Paint her, mad and old and abandoned.
Paint Artaud in grey marble.
Paint Latimbrée reciting your poems.
Paint René, profoundly intoxicated.
Paint yourself, your loving gaze toward my furi-
ous eyes.
And paint me, proud, strong, my pockets full of pis-
tols, making a big *pow* before getting assassinated."
She said, "Paint us a bit out of focus, a bit wrong, for
nostalgia's sake, to make it more endearing.
Paint our rebellion, our madness, our pain. Us. It has
to mean something."

> *A pow is heard. Very brief blackout, perhaps a
> camera flash… We return and everyone is frozen
> as if in* PAZ's *painting.* PAZ *is front and centre,
> loaded down with pistols.*

Translator's Notes

1) In the original French, June's periodic lapses into English (complete with a few Anglo-Saxon swear words, which have slightly less force to a French-speaking ear) rendered her speech somewhat coarser than that of the other characters. Since June bursting into French would have the exact opposite effect, she is instead set apart here by her use of period American slang laced with profanities. It's important to note, however, that June is a Bohemian, not a gangster's moll, and is written with a distinctive mix of vulgarity and refinement.

2) When Anaïs was assaulted by Fred, she declared (in the French) that she was "*inviolable.*" On one level, this word means the same as in English: something "not to be violated, broken, or profaned" (Canadian Oxford Dictionary). However, since *viol* is the normal everyday French word for "rape," there's a visceral punch to the word Anaïs speaks while she is, in fact, being violated. That is why, in this version, she creates her own word: "unrapable."

Further Reading

Artaud, Antonin. *Artaud Anthology*. Translation by Jack Hirschman. San Francisco: City Lights, 2001.

———. *Oeuvres*. Paris: Quarto Gallimard, 2004.

———. *The Theater and Its Double*. Translation by Mary Caroline Richards. New York: Grove, 1994.

———. *Le théâtre et son double*. Paris: Gallimard, 1964.

Gautrand, Jean-Claude. *Brassaï, 1899–1984*. Paris: Taschen, 2004.

Nin, Anaïs. *Henry and June: From "A Journal of Love"—The Unexpurgated Diary of Anaïs Nin (1931–1932)*. Boston: Harcourt, 1990.

———. *Henry et June, Cahiers secrets volume 1*. Paris: Édition Le Cercle, 2006.

———. *Incest: From "A Journal of Love"—The Unexpurgated Diary of Anaïs Nin (1932–1934)*. Boston: Mariner Books, 1993.

———. *Inceste: Journal inédit et non expurgé des années 1932–1934, (tiré du Journal de l'Amour)*. Traduit de l'anglais par Béatrice Commengé. Édition le livre de poche, 2002.

Catherine Léger has written for theatre, television, and film. Her plays include *Voiture américaine, Princesses,* and the short pieces *Chevreuil, Perdus/Lost,* and *Catfight.* She was a writer for the Radio-Canada TV series *La job* and *Toc toc toc.* She also co-wrote with Sophie Lorain the film *Le Temps des Roses.*

Leanna Brodie is an actor, writer, and the translator of several plays, including Sébastien Harrisson's *From Alaska*, Hélène Ducharme's *Baobab*, and Louise Bombardier's *My Mother Dog*. She has also written the CBC Radio dramas *Invisible City* and *Seeds of Our Destruction* as well as the stage plays *The Vic, For Home and Country, Schoolhouse*, and *The Book of Esther* (published by Talonbooks) and opera libretti such as *Ulla's Odyssey* (with New Zealand composer Anthony Young). She is playwright-in-residence at Lighthouse Festival Theatre and at the 4th Line Theatre.